For
Every Child

For Every Child

The UN Convention on the Rights of the Child
in words and pictures

Text adapted by Caroline Castle

Published in association with UNICEF

RED FOX

Foreword

In this book you will see many pictures of children as they should be — happy, healthy, laughing, learning, holding securely to adults they could trust, who would protect and uphold their inalienable rights — the rights formally laid out in the UN Convention on the Rights of the Child. These are the rights of all children everywhere and always.

During the Vietnam War, we were shocked by a picture that flashed round the world. It was of a young Vietnamese girl running and screaming. She was naked and ablaze, the target of napalm bombing. The picture captured the ghastliness of war and showed dramatically that the vast bulk of victims of war were innocent unarmed civilians, mainly women and children and the elderly — totally unacceptable targets of the weapons of death and destruction even if they were camouflaged as 'collateral damage'. They were non-combatants, the vulnerable whom all the conventions governing the conduct of war pronounced as untouchable, a protected species — provisions of those conventions kept far more in the breach than in the observance.

A little later the world saw another picture that was flashed on TV screens and made the pages of most newspapers. It showed a black young man and a black young woman carrying the limp body of a small black boy who had been shot (he died a little later, so the first fatality) by the South African police as young blacks revolted against the oppression and injustice of apartheid, South Africa's vicious racist system, in the Soweto uprising of 16 June 1976.

There have been other pictures to appal us, showing children as they should not be, hollow eyed and potbellied, as victims of malnutrition, famine and disease; as bewildered refugees fleeing from the violations of their fundamental human rights to a secure home environment, with a country they could call their own. We have seen pictures of children benumbed after witnessing the mass killings of relatives, of parents mown down before their very eyes, children abused and raped and taught to kill as child soldiers, perhaps the ultimate obscenity, when they should have been laughing and playing instead of being trained to mutilate and made to carry guns grotesquely too large for their childish hands.

We are at the beginning of a new millennium. Let us commit ourselves to outlaw the conditions that have made the second kind of pictures possible. The 20th century has been noted for its conflict, bloodshed and strife. Let the 21st century be marked by peace and justice and development. Let us do everything in our power to promote the conditions that make the first kind of pictures, those found in this book, possible.

We each can make a difference if we are vigilant to create a new kind of society, more compassionate, more caring, more sharing where human rights, where children's rights are respected and protected. Politicians ultimately offer what the people want. Let us tell them we want peace and prosperity for everyone.

Start today. God bless you in the New Millennium.

Archbishop Desmond M. Tutu

Whoever we are, wherever we live, these rights belong to all children under the sun and the moon and the stars, whether we live in cities or towns or villages, or in mountains or valleys or deserts or forests

or jungles. Anywhere and everywhere in the big, wide world, these are the rights of every child.

Right No. 2 illustrated by Rachel Isadora

Understand that all children are precious. Pick us up if we fall down and if we are lost lend us your hand. Give us the things we need to

make us happy and strong, and always do your best for us whenever
we are in your care.

Right No. 3 illustrated by Henriette Sauvant

All children should be allowed to live and to grow ... and grow ... and grow ... until we are grown up and can decide things for ourselves.

Right No. 6 illustrated by Babette Cole

Max, Zahra, Betty, Juan, Suyin, Reza, Paolo, Yair, Yoko, Mohammed . . .
Every one of us shall have a name and a land to call our own.

Right No. 7 illustrated by Jerry Pinkney

Keep our families together, and if we have no family, look after us and
love us just the same.

Right No. 9 illustrated by Ken Wilson-Max

Allow us to tell you what we are thinking or feeling. Whether our voices are big or small; whether we whisper or shout it, or paint,

draw, mime or sign it – listen to us and hear what we say.

Right No. 13 illustrated by John Burningham

No one on Earth has the right to hurt us, not even our mums and dads. Protect us always from anyone who would be cruel.

Right No. 19 illustrated by Claudio Muñoz

If we are disabled, either in body or in mind, treasure us especially
and give us the care we need to live happily in the world.

Right No. 23 illustrated by Peter Weevers

Watch over us. Wrap us up against the cold and rain, and give us shade from the hot sun. Make sure we have enough to eat and drink

and if we are sick, nurse and comfort us.

Right No. 24 illustrated by P. J. Lynch

Teach us all to read and write and teach us well so we grow up to be the best we can at whatever we wish to do. Take care of our Earth –

the flowers, the trees, the rivers, the seas – and teach us how to care
for it in our turn.

Rights No. 28 & 29 illustrated by Satoshi Kitamura

All children shall have time to play and time to rest when we are tired.

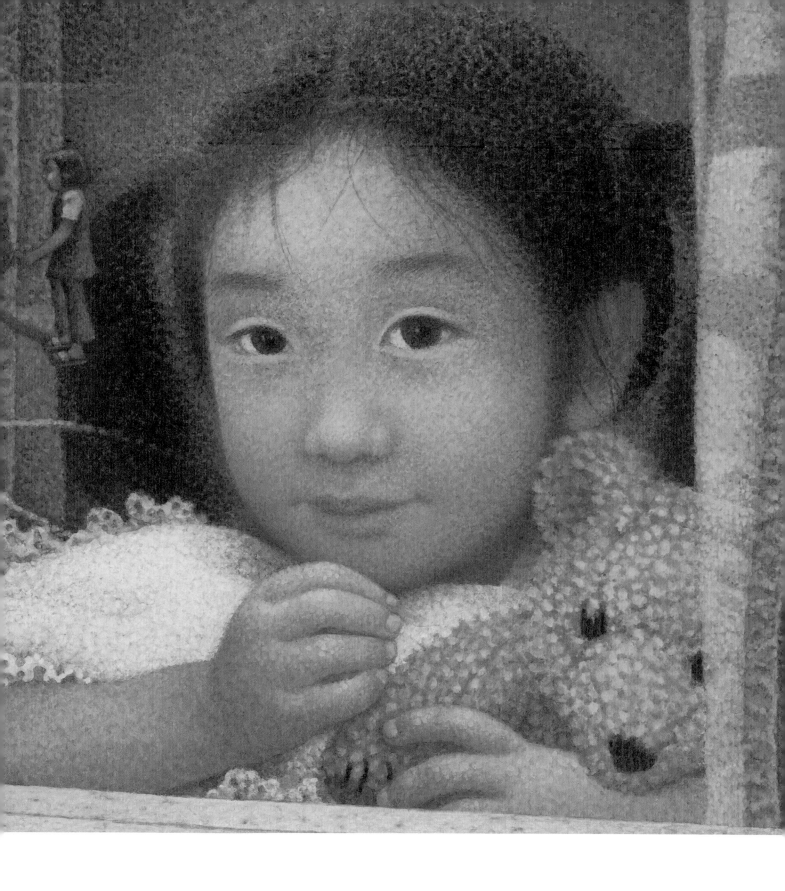

Right No. 31 illustrated by Yang Tswei-yu

In times of war do not make us part of any battle, but shelter us and protect us from all harm.

Right No. 38 illustrated by Shirley Hughes

Allow us to say our own prayers in our own words, whether in churches or temples, synagogues or mosques, chapels or shrines

or any other place a prayer may be said to our own God. And let us sing and dance and dress in the ways of our own people.

Right No. 30 illustrated by Rabindra and Amrit K.D. Kaur Singh

Do your best to let everyone know that, whoever we are, wherever we live, these are the rights of every child.

Right No. 42 illustrated by Philippe Dumas

ILLUSTRATORS

John Burningham

John Burningham was born in Farnham, Surrey, and graduated from the Central School of Art in London. His first book, *Borka: The Adventures of a Goose With No Feathers*, published in 1963, won the Kate Greenaway Medal. Many other books followed, including *Mr Gumpy's Outing*, another Greenaway Medal winner, and *Granpa*, winner of the Emil/Kurt Maschler Award. *Granpa* and *Oi, Get Off Our Train* have been made into successful animated films.

Medium used: pencil, watercolour and ink

Philippe Dumas

Philippe Dumas was born in France and now lives in Switzerland. He has been writing and illustrating children's books for many years. His titles include *Odette: A Springtime in Paris* by Kay Fender, *The Scarlet Ibis* by James Hurst, *The Queen Bee* by the Brothers Grimm, *Laura Alice's New Puppy*, *The Story of Edward* and, most recently, *A Farm*. His books have won many awards; in 1987 he was awarded the Grand Prix de Littérature Enfantine by the City of Paris in recognition of his work.

Medium used: pastel and watercolour

Babette Cole

Babette Cole was born in the Channel Islands and graduated from Canterbury College of Art. Her first book was published in 1976 and she has since written and illustrated over 70 titles. These include *Mummy Laid an Egg*, published in 1993 and winner of the British Book Awards Book of the Year, *Hair in Funny Places*, short-listed for their Children's Book of the Year in 2000, *Prince Cinders*, runner-up for the Smarties Prize, *Princess Smartypants* and *Two of Everything*.

Medium used: pastel, watercolour and crayon

Shirley Hughes

Shirley Hughes was born and grew up near Liverpool. She trained at the Liverpool Art School and at the Ruskin School of Art, Oxford, where she later became a visiting tutor. Her first book, *Lucy and Tom's Day*, was published in 1960, and she has now illustrated over 200 books for children. *Dogger*, published in 1977, won both the Kate Greenaway Medal and the Dutch Silver Pencil Medal. Shirley received the Eleanor Farjeon Award for her distinguished services to children and books, and was awarded the OBE in 1999.

Medium used: gouache and oil pastel

Rachel Isadora

Rachel Isadora was born and raised in New York City. She worked as a professional ballet dancer before turning to illustrating children's books full time. She is the author/illustrator of many books, including *Ben's Trumpet*, which received the Caldecott Honour Award and the Boston Globe/Horn Book Honour Award, *Lili at Ballet*, *Opening Night*, *At the Crossroads*, *Caribbean Dreams* and *ABC POP*.

Medium used: watercolour

Satoshi Kitamura

Satoshi Kitamura was born in Tokyo. His first picture book, *Angry Arthur*, with words by Hiawyn Oram, won the 1983 Mother Goose Award. He has collaborated with Oram on other titles including *In the Attic* and *A Boy Meets a Dinosaur*. He has also successfully collaborated with poet John Agard on the collection, *We Animals Would Like A Word With You*, and is both author and illustrator of *Sheep in Wolves' Clothing*, *When Sheep Cannot Sleep*, *U.F.O. Diary* and *Me and My Cat*, among other titles.

Medium used: watercolour

P.J. Lynch

P.J. Lynch was born in Belfast and now lives in Dublin. He studied at Brighton College of Art, where his tutors included John Vernon Lord and Raymond Briggs. His first book, *A Bag of Moonshine* by Alan Garner, won the 1987 Mother Goose Award. He is a two-time winner of the Kate Greenaway Medal for *The Christmas Miracle of Jonathan Toomey* by Susan Wojciechowski, which also won the Reading Association of Ireland Award, and for *When Jessie Came Across the Sea* by Amy Hest. He has provided illustrations for E. Nesbit's *Melisande* and Oscar Wilde's *Stories for Children*, among other titles.

Medium used: watercolour and gouache

Claudio Muñoz

Claudio Muñoz was born and raised in Chile. He studied architecture at university before turning to children's illustration. *Big Baby*, his first book, was runner-up for the Mother Goose Award in 1987. Other books include *Come Back, Grandma*, runner-up for the Smarties Prize in 1994, *Little Captain*, winner of the Prix du Livre de la Mer in 1997 and *Nobody Likes Me* with words by Fay Weldon.

Medium used: china ink and watercolour

Jerry Pinkney

Jerry Pinkney, a native of Philadelphia, Pennsylvania, studied at the Philadelphia College of Art. He has been illustrating children's books since 1964, and has published over 80 titles. He has the rare distinction of being the recipient of three Caldecott Honour Medals: in 1989 for *Mirandy and Brother Wind*, in 1990 for *The Talking Eggs* and in 1995 for *John Henry*. He has won the Coretta Scott King Award four times and a Coretta Scott King Honour twice. In addition to his children's books, he has exhibited his work at galleries and museums throughout the world and has held professorships at the Pratt Institute, the University of Delaware and the University at Buffalo.

Medium used: watercolour and pencil

Rabindra and Amrit K.D. Kaur Singh

Rabindra and Amrit K.D. Kaur Singh are twin sisters based in Merseyside. They began exhibiting in 1987 and their award-winning work has appeared in shows at leading UK venues, including the National Portrait Gallery and the Whitechapel Gallery in London, as well as in Switzerland, Germany and France. They have work in national collections around Britain. Their publications include *Bindhu's Weddings*, a children's book of poems about Asian weddings in Britain, and *Twin Perspectives*, a book profiling their work.

Medium used: gouache

Henriette Sauvant

Henriette Sauvant was born in Bonn, Germany. She received a diploma in children's book illustration in Hamburg. Her first book, *The Seven Ravens*, was published in 1995, followed by *Allerleirauh* and *Hello, Is Someone There?* with words by Jostein Gaarder. She has been nominated for the German Youth Prize for Literature, as well as for the Pied Piper Prize for Literature.

Medium used: oil

Peter Weevers

Peter Weevers was born in Essex. His first picture book, *The Hare and the Tortoise*, was published in 1984. It received the Children's Books Selectors' Award and was chosen as one of the Books of the Year in 1986 by the Child Study Association of America. Other titles include *Herbert Binns and The Flying Tricycle*, *The March Hare*, *The Christmas Fox*, *Alice's Adventures in Wonderland* and *The Pied Piper of Hamelin*.

Medium used: watercolour, pencil and ink

Ken Wilson-Max

Ken Wilson-Max was born in Harare, Zimbabwe. He studied and worked as a designer before turning to children's illustration full time. His books include *Big Yellow Taxi*, *Little Red Plane*, *Wake Up, Sleep Tight*, *The Sun is a Bright Star*, *Best Friends in the Snow*, *Tic Tac Toe (Three in a Row)* and *Dexter Gets Dressed*.

Medium used: acrylic

Yang Tswei-yu

Yang Tswei-yu was born in Taipei, where she still lives. She attended the Fu Shin Art School there. Her books include *The Son's Big Toy*, *Li Tien Luo* and *Tainan, the Old Town*. She was selected to take part in the 30th Annual Illustrators' Exhibition at Bologna in 1996.

Medium used: acrylic

The Rights Featured in this Book from The UN Convention on the Rights of the Child

ARTICLE 2: *Non-discrimination*

1. States Parties shall respect and ensure the rights set forth in the present Convention to each child within their jurisdiction without discrimination of any kind, irrespective of the child's or his or her parent's or legal guardian's race, colour, sex, language, religion, political or other opinion, national, ethnic or social origin, property, disability, birth or other status.

2. States Parties shall take all appropriate measures to ensure that the child is protected against all forms of discrimination or punishment on the basis of the status, activities, expressed opinions, or beliefs of the child's parents, legal guardians, or family members.

ARTICLE 3: *Best interests of the child*

1. In all actions concerning children, whether undertaken by public or private social welfare institutions, courts of law, administrative authorities or legislative bodies, the best interests of the child shall be a primary consideration.

2. States Parties undertake to ensure the child such protection and care as is necessary for his or her well-being, taking into account the rights and duties of his or her parents, legal guardians, or other individuals legally responsible for him or her, and, to this end, shall take all appropriate legislative and administrative measures.

3. States Parties shall ensure that the institutions, services and facilities responsible for the care or protection of children shall conform with the standards established by competent authorities, particularly in the areas of safety, health, in the number and suitability of their staff as well as competent supervision.

ARTICLE 6: *Survival and development*

1. States Parties recognise that every child has the inherent right to life.
2. States Parties shall ensure to the maximum extent possible the survival and development of the child.

ARTICLE 7: *Name and nationality*

1. The child shall be registered immediately after birth and shall have the right from birth to a name, the right to acquire a nationality and, as far as possible, the right to know and be cared for by his or her parents.

2. States Parties shall ensure the implementation of these rights in accordance with their national law and their obligations under the relevant international instruments in this field, in particular where the child would otherwise be stateless.

ARTICLE 9: *Separation from parents*

1. States Parties shall ensure that the child shall not be separated from his or her parents against their will, except when competent authorities subject to judicial review determine, in accordance with applicable law and procedures, that such separation is necessary for the best interests of the child. Such determination may be necessary in a particular case such as one involving abuse or neglect of the child by the parents, or one where the parents are living separately and a decision must be made as to the child's place of residence.

2. In any proceeding pursuant to paragraph 1 of the present article, all interested parties shall be given an opportunity to participate in the proceedings and make their views known.

3. States Parties shall respect the right of the child who is separated from one or both parents to maintain personal relations and direct contact with both parents on a regular basis, except if it is contrary to the child's best interests.

4. Where such separation results from any action initiated by a State Party, such as the detention, imprisonment, exile, deportation or death (including death arising from any cause while the person is in custody of the State) of one or both parents or of the child, that State Party shall, upon request, provide the parents, the child or, if appropriate, another member of the family with the essential information concerning the whereabouts of the absent member(s) of the family unless the provision of the information would be detrimental to the well-being of the child. States Parties shall further ensure that the submission of such a request shall of itself entail no adverse consequences for the person(s) concerned.

ARTICLE 13: *Freedom of expression*

1. The child shall have the right to freedom of expression; this right shall include the freedom to seek, receive and impart information and ideas of all kinds, regardless of frontiers, either orally, in writing or in print, in the form of art, or through any other media of the child's choice.

2. The exercise of this right may be subject to certain restrictions, but these shall only be such as are provided by law and are necessary:
   (a) For respect of the rights or reputations of others; or
   (b) For the protection of national security or of public order (*ordre public*), or of public health or morals.

ARTICLE 19: *Protection from abuse and neglect*

1. States Parties shall take all appropriate legislative, administrative, social and educational measures to protect the child from all forms of physical or mental violence, injury or abuse, neglect or negligent treatment, maltreatment or exploitation, including sexual abuse, while in the care of parent(s), legal guardian(s) or any other person who has the care of a child.

2. Such protective measures should, as appropriate, include effective procedures for the establishment of social programmes to provide necessary support for the child and for those who have the care of the child, as well as for other forms of prevention and for identification, reporting, referral, investigation, treatment and follow-up of instances of child maltreatment described heretofore, and, as appropriate, for judicial involvement.

ARTICLE 23: *Disabled children*

1. States Parties recognise that a mentally or physically disabled child should enjoy a full and decent life, in conditions which ensure dignity, promote self-reliance, and facilitate the child's active participation in the community.

2. States Parties recognise the right of the disabled child to special care and shall encourage and ensure the extension, subject to available resources, to the eligible child and those responsible for his or her care, of assistance for which application is made and which is appropriate to the child's condition and to the circumstances of the parents or others caring for the child.

3. Recognising the special needs of a disabled child, assistance extended in accordance with paragraph 2 of the present article shall be provided free of charge, whenever possible, taking into account the financial resources of the parents or others caring for the child, and shall be designed to ensure that the disabled child has effective access to and receives education, training, health care services, rehabilitation services, preparation for employment and recreation opportunities in a manner conducive to the child's achieving the fullest possible social integration and individual development, including his or her cultural and spiritual development.

4. States Parties shall promote, in the spirit of international co-operation, the exchange of appropriate information in the field of preventive health care and of medical, psychological and functional treatment of disabled children,

including dissemination of and access to information concerning methods of rehabilitation, education and vocational services, with the aim of enabling States Parties to improve their capabilities and skills and to widen their experience in these areas. In this regard, particular account shall be taken of the needs of developing countries.

ARTICLE 24: *Health and health services*

1. States Parties recognise the right of the child to the enjoyment of the highest attainable standard of health and to facilities for the treatment of illness and rehabilitation of health. States Parties shall strive to ensure that no child is deprived of his or her right of access to such health care services.
2. States Parties shall pursue full implementation of this right and, in particular, shall take appropriate measures:
   (a) To diminish infant and child mortality;
   (b) To ensure the provision of necessary medical assistance and health care to all children with emphasis on the development of primary health care;
   (c) To combat disease and malnutrition, including within the framework of primary health care, through, *inter alia*, the application of readily available technology and through the provision of adequate nutritious foods and clean drinking-water, taking into consideration the dangers and risks of environmental pollution;
   (d) To ensure appropriate pre-natal and post-natal health care for mothers;
   (e) To ensure that all segments of society, in particular parents and children, are informed, have access to education and are supported in the use of basic knowledge of child health and nutrition, the advantages of breast-feeding, hygiene and environmental sanitation and the prevention of accidents;
   (f) To develop preventive health care, guidance for parents, and family planning education and services.
3. States Parties shall take all effective and appropriate measures with a view to abolishing traditional practices prejudicial to the health of children.
4. States Parties undertake to promote and encourage international co-operation with a view to achieving progressively the full realisation of the right recognised in the present article. In this regard, particular account shall be taken of the needs of developing countries.

ARTICLE 28: *Education*

1. States Parties recognise the right of the child to education, and with a view to achieving this right progressively and on the basis of equal opportunity, they shall, in particular:
   (a) Make primary education compulsory and available free to all;
   (b) Encourage the development of different forms of secondary education, including general and vocational education, make them available and accessible to every child, and take appropriate measures such as the introduction of free education and offering financial assistance in case of need;
   (c) Make higher education accessible to all on the basis of capacity by every appropriate means;
   (d) Make educational and vocational information and guidance available and accessible to all children;
   (e) Take measures to encourage regular attendance at schools and the reduction of drop-out rates.
2. States Parties shall take all appropriate measures to ensure that school discipline is administered in a manner consistent with the child's human dignity and in conformity with the present Convention.
3. States Parties shall promote and encourage international co-operation in matters relating to education, in particular with a view to contributing to the elimination of ignorance and illiteracy throughout the world and facilitating access to scientific and technical knowledge and modern teaching methods. In this regard, particular account shall be taken of the needs of developing countries.

ARTICLE 29: *Aims of education*

1. States Parties agree that the education of the child shall be directed to:
   (a) The development of the child's personality, talents and mental and physical abilities to their fullest potential;
   (b) The development of respect for human rights and fundamental freedoms, and for the principles enshrined in the Charter of the United Nations;
   (c) The development of respect for the child's parents, his or her own cultural identity, language and values, for the national values of the country in which the child is living, the country from which he or she may originate, and for civilisations different from his or her own;
   (d) The preparation of the child for responsible life in a free society, in the spirit of understanding, peace, tolerance, equality of sexes, and friendship among all peoples, ethnic, national and religious groups and persons of indigenous origin;
   (e) The development of respect for the natural environment.
2. No part of the present article or article 28 shall be construed so as to interfere with the liberty of individuals and bodies to establish and direct educational institutions, subject always to the observance of these principles set forth in paragraph 1 of the present article and to the requirements that the education given in such institutions shall conform to such minimum standards as may be laid down by the State.

ARTICLE 30: *Children of minorities or indigenous peoples*

In those States in which ethnic, religious or linguistic minorities or persons of indigenous origin exist, a child belonging to such a minority or who is indigenous shall not be denied the right, in community with other members of his or her group, to enjoy his or her own culture, to profess and practise his or her own religion, or to use his or her own language.

ARTICLE 31: *Leisure, recreation and cultural activities*

1. States Parties recognise the right of the child to rest and leisure, to engage in play and recreational activities appropriate to the age of the child and to participate freely in cultural life and the arts.
2. States Parties shall respect and promote the right of the child to participate fully in cultural and artistic life and shall encourage the provision of appropriate and equal opportunities for cultural, artistic, recreational and leisure activity.

ARTICLE 38: *Armed conflicts*

1. States Parties undertake to respect and to ensure respect for rules of international humanitarian law applicable to them in armed conflicts which are relevant to the child.
2. States Parties shall take all feasible measures to ensure that persons who have not attained the age of fifteen years do not take a direct part in hostilities.
3. States Parties shall refrain from recruiting any person who has not attained the age of fifteen years into their armed forces. In recruiting among those persons who have attained the age of fifteen years but who have not attained the age of eighteen years, States Parties shall endeavour to give priority to those who are oldest.
4. In accordance with their obligations under international humanitarian law to protect the civilian population in armed conflicts, States Parties shall take all feasible measures to ensure the protection and care of children who are affected by an armed conflict.

ARTICLE 42

States Parties undertake to make the principles and provisions of the Convention widely known, by appropriate and active means, to adults and children alike.

For Every Child

A RED FOX BOOK 978 0 099 40865 9

First published in Great Britain by Hutchinson,
an imprint of Random House Children's Publishers UK

Hutchinson edition published 2000
Red Fox edition published 2002

16 18 20 19 17 15

Red Fox Books are published by Random House Children's Publishers UK,
61–63 Uxbridge Road, London W5 5SA,
a division of The Random House Group Ltd.
Addresses for companies within The Random House Group Limited can
be found at:www.randomhouse.co.uk/offices.htm

THE RANDOM HOUSE GROUP Limited Reg. No. 954009
www.randomhousechildrens.co.uk

A CIP catalogue record for this book is available from the British Library.

Printed in China by Midas Printing Ltd